Why don't you get a *horse,*

SAM ADAMS?

by Jean Fritz

illustrated by Trina Schart Hyman

COWARD, McCANN & GEOGHEGAN, Inc.
NEW YORK

To Jean Whitnack

In the early days of America when men wore ruffles on their shirts and buckles on their shoes, when they rode horseback and swore allegiance to the King of England, there lived in Boston a man who cared for none of these things. His name was Samuel Adams. His clothes were shabby and plain, he refused to get on a horse, and he hated the King of England.

Samuel Adams was known as a talker and a walker. Six days of the week he would walk about Boston, talking to anyone who would listen—talking about England, always about England. What he thought about was independence, but it was a long time before he dared say "independence" out loud. Americans were still loyal to the king, even though they were often angry at the way England treated its colonies. And Samuel Adams made it his business to keep the people angry.

From one end of the town to another Samuel walked. Indeed, how else was he to travel? A man cannot say much
from the top of a horse except good morning, good evening,
or giddyap, and Samuel Adams had a great deal more than
that to say. Still, he did not travel alone. At his side was
Queue, his shaggy Newfoundland dog.

Together they went to the docks, and while Samuel Adams talked to merchants about the wrongs of the English government, Queue smelled the good smells of Boston Harbor—drying codfish, wet rope, and sometimes, if he was lucky, a giant turtle in a crate shipped up from the South. (New Englanders doted on turtle soup.)

Together Samuel and Queue called on shopkeepers. Generally Samuel went inside and talked about the wickedness of England; generally Queue stayed outside and chased a stray chicken or stopped at a hitching post to visit with a horse.

Together Samuel and Queue would drop in at a tavern. Samuel would sit down and talk about American rights; Queue, blinking through the hair that fell over his eyes, would search the floor for crumbs—a morsel of cheese, a bite of plumcake, and sometimes, if he was lucky, a discarded bone.

Samuel's younger cousin John Adams often became impatient with all his walking. "Why don't you learn to ride a horse?" he would ask.

11

But Samuel would not learn. Winter and summer he walked and he talked. Indeed, he paid so little attention to his private business that he became quite poor. His house fell into disrepair; his clothes became shabbier; his shoe leather wore thin.

Meanwhile, England was imposing taxes on America. First a stamp tax on printed matter. No one could obtain a marriage license now or a college diploma or even buy a newspaper without paying England a share of the money. This made the people of Boston so angry they tore down the governor's house, set fire to the tax office, and elected Samuel Adams a representative to the Massachusetts legislature.

Being a member of the government, Samuel had a chance to talk to more people, but still he walked. Even when England withdrew the stamp tax, Samuel talked and walked, warning the merchants and the shopkeepers and the people at the taverns not to trust England. It had taxed America once, he said; it would try it again. And indeed a year later it did. This time Americans had to give England money whenever they bought paint, glass, lead, or tea. This made the people so angry that the king decided to send soldiers to Boston to keep order.

They arrived in Boston on October 1, 1768—two regiments
of soldiers in red coats. From the harbor they marched—one
thousand strong, their drums beating, fifes playing, flags fly-
ing, and bayonets fixed. They marched straight to Boston
Common, a park in the center of town where people were
accustomed to take walks, play games, and graze their cows.
There the soldiers set up tents and settled down for the winter.

It was a long winter. Every time he turned around, it seemed to Samuel Adams, there was a redcoat. He woke up hearing redcoats drill; he went to bed hearing their bugles. Redcoats stopped him on his walks to ask his name and business. Samuel Adams longed for America to fight the redcoats then and there, but he knew the country was not ready yet for war or independence.

But Queue could fight. Under Samuel's careful training, Queue learned to hate redcoats. He growled and snarled when they passed; he barked and snapped when they came near. And sometimes, if he was lucky, he came home with a piece of red cloth in his mouth.

Meanwhile, Samuel kept on talking and walking.

"Why can't you ride a horse like everyone else?" his cousin John asked.

But Samuel shook his head.

Twice in the next few years Americans came close to fighting.

Once a mob of young men swung clubs and threw rock-filled snowballs at the redcoats until the redcoats finally fired back. (Samuel Adams did his fiercest talking against the redcoats in this instance.)

Another time a band of men, dressed up like Indians, dumped a boatload of tea into Boston Harbor rather than see the tea taxed. (Samuel was the one who gave the signal to go down to the docks.)

By the fall of 1774 Americans were so alarmed about England that they called a meeting in Philadelphia to discuss what to do. Samuel Adams was chosen to go as one of the representatives from Massachusetts. He had never been out of Massachusetts before.

"You are now a traveler," his friends pointed out, "and you should learn to ride a horse."

But Samuel said that would not be necessary; the representatives were going to Philadelphia in a coach. He stood before his friends, his coat frayed, his shoes scuffed, his cotton stockings darned. His friends said nothing about his appearance, but within a few day gifts began arriving at his house:

1 maroon-colored broadcloth suit
6 pairs of buckled shoes
6 pairs of white silk stockings
2 ruffled shirts
1 wig

When Samuel Adams left for Philadelphia, he was dressed as a representative of Massachusetts should be dressed. He was as stylish as his cousin John Adams, or his friend John Hancock, or indeed any of the other representatives. And if the others could ride a horse and he couldn't, he didn't care.

Actually, it was lucky that Samuel could at least look nice because he couldn't say much at the meeting. Many of the representatives from other colonies still weren't ready for talk about independence so Samuel had to be patient awhile longer. There was a time, he knew, for throwing snowballs and a time for dumping tea, but there was also a time for sitting still under your new wig and holding your tongue. This was such a time.

But of course he couldn't be still forever. By 1775 Samuel was talking openly of independence. He was fifty-three years old now and at the top of the king's "most wanted" list of American traitors. John Hancock was on the list, too. As for Queue, unfortunately he was dead. He had fought his last battle with the redcoats before the real fighting began.

On April 18 the redcoats marched out of Boston, looking for American cannon that was hidden in Concord and looking (so it was said) for Samuel Adams and John Hancock,

who were hidden in a friend's house in Lexington. Samuel wasn't afraid of trouble. The more trouble there was with the redcoats, the sooner Americans would be willing to declare their independence and the better he'd like it. But of course, he preferred not to be caught.

Fortunately for Samuel and John, the Americans had discovered what the English were up to. Ahead of the redcoats rode Paul Revere. He galloped up to the house where Samuel Adams and John Hancock were staying.

"The redcoats are coming!" he cried.

Samuel jumped out of bed, ready to fly for his life. (He was in such a hurry that he left his watch under his pillow.) John also jumped out of bed, but he was more eager to fight than to fly. He grabbed his sword and began to polish it.

Samuel told him to put his sword away. "We aren't meant to be soldiers," he said. "We are the brains behind the Revolution. It is our duty to escape."

Reluctantly John put his sword away and made ready to escape. Now, of course, as everyone knows, the way to escape from an enemy is on the back of a horse. You lean forward and with hooves thundering behind, you streak into the night. But Samuel Adams couldn't ride a horse.

In the end there was nothing for John Hancock to do but call for his carriage and his driver. The two men took their seats and rolled sedately away to a neighboring town. (Eventually they found a swamp to hide in.) It was not a heroic escape, but it was an escape. The only thing Samuel Adams regretted was that he'd left his watch behind.

Even now he would not ride a horse.

In September on the way to another meeting in Philadelphia, John Adams tried again to persuade him. This time they were traveling alone—John and Samuel and their two servants. John and his servant, Fessenden, were on horses; Samuel and his servant were in a two-wheeled chaise. Under such cir-

cumstances, it was hard for John and Samuel to talk. John suggested that Samuel could ride Fessenden's horse and Fessenden could get in the chaise. Samuel suggested that his servant could ride John's horse and John could get in the chaise, but John loved to ride. So John trotted along to Philadelphia, and Samuel rolled along, each with his own thoughts.

JOHN HANCOCK'S FLINTLOCK RIFLE (USED)

It took a week or more to go from Boston to Philadelphia, but of course there were many stops at inns, where John and Samuel could talk together. And there was much to talk about. Since the Battle of Lexington, George Washington had been put in command of an American army and there had been another battle at Bunker Hill. But there wasn't enough time to talk about all that had happened and was still to happen to the country.

At a tavern in Grafton, Connecticut, John Adams decided to make one last attempt to get Samuel on a horse.

"Riding would be good for your health," he began.

Samuel was not concerned with his health.

Riding was sociable, John suggested. Samuel said walking was sociable and riding in a chaise could be sociable, too.

Well, riding was a more convenient way to get about, John went on. As a leader of the Revolution, Samuel was a busy man and needed to get about easily.

Samuel was not interested in convenience.

Riding was the fastest way to travel, John observed. In time of war, it was sometimes important to move fast.

JOHN ADAMS'S SWORD (NEVER USED IN BATTLE)

Still, Samuel was not convinced. If he thought about his escape at Lexington, he didn't mention it.

John sighed and tried another tack. It was a pity, he said, that early man had gone to such trouble to domesticate an animal, only to have Samuel Adams come along and reject it.

Samuel didn't give two hoots for early man.

Then John Adams sat back in his chair and took a deep breath. He had one more argument. "You should ride a horse for the good of your country," he declared. America would surely be declaring its independence soon, he pointed out; if all went well, they themselves would be signing such a declaration in Philadelphia. Then they would be not just leaders of a revolution; they would be the statesmen of a new nation.

John leaned toward his cousin. "A proud new nation," he said. A great nation. A republic as Rome had been in ancient times. And whoever heard of a great nation with statesmen who could not ride horseback? John listed the heroes of Roman history. He reviewed the names of Roman senators. All were horsemen, he said. And he would not want Americans to be inferior in the least way.

For the first time Samuel looked thoughtful. After all, he told himself, he had put on silk stockings and a ruffled shirt so as not to shame the Commonwealth of Massachusetts at the meeting in Philadelphia. How could he refuse to get on a horse if the honor of his country were at stake? How could he put a stain on American history—indeed right on the opening chapter?

Samuel closed his eyes and tried to imagine the new nation

that John described. Yes, it seemed to him that he could see it—people multiplying, buildings springing up, roads unrolling. And stone statues popping up across the landscape. They were statues of the new nation's first statesmen, and they were all on horseback. There was John Adams in stone on a horse. And John Hancock. There were dozens of George Washingtons on dozens of horses. But try as he might, Samuel could not find a statue of himself. If he did not ride a horse, he asked himself, would he not even be granted a pedestal?

When they were ready to continue the journey, Samuel
walked over to Fessenden's horse. He eyed it suspiciously.

"She is a very gentle creature," John assured him.

Samuel said nothing, but he allowed the two servants to
boost him onto the horse. He listened to John's instructions.
He did as he was told. Then the servants rolled along to Philadelphia in the chaise, and Samuel and John rode together.

Everyone agreed that Samuel did remarkably well in the saddle. There was only one trouble. At the end of the day it was discovered that at the place where Samuel Adams and the saddle met Samuel was sore. And everyone agreed that this was no way for a future statesman to feel. So at Woodstock, Connecticut, where they spent the night, John bought two yards of flannel, found a tailor, and ordered a pair of padded underpants, or "drawers," for Samuel.

The next morning John gave Samuel his final lesson in horse-manship. A statesman, he explained, should not have to be hoisted and heaved into the saddle by two servants. He should be able to mount himself.

He told Samuel to grasp the bridle with his right hand over the pummel of the saddle, to place his left foot in the stirrup, to twist his left hand into the horse's mane halfway between his ears and his shoulders, and, propelling himself upward, to throw his right leg over the saddle. Samuel did as he was told.

44

So mounted, in his padded drawers, Samuel rode triumphantly to Philadelphia, the very picture of a noble statesman.

And when independence was finally declared one hot July day ten months later, Samuel Adams was ready for history.

SAM

For those readers who will ask if the facts in this book are true, the answer is *yes*. I was disappointed that there was no more information to be found about Queue, but I am grateful to John Adams for telling us in such detail about how Samuel Adams finally learned to ride a horse. On September 17, 1775, John wrote all about it, including the specific instructions for mounting a horse given on page 42, in a letter to his friend James Warren.

For those readers who would like to know more about Samuel Adams, here are some additional facts.

Samuel Adams' anger at England started early in his life. His father, a wealthy and prominent businessman, was at the center of a political movement that wanted to give more power to the American people and less to England. Samuel was eighteen and a student at Harvard University when a new bank that his father and his friends had started suddenly failed. Samuel's father lost so much money that in order to pay his way through college, Samuel had to take a job waiting on table. Samuel didn't mind the job; he never cared about having money for himself, but the bank had failed because England had declared it illegal and in a way that many people thought was unfair. This was what Samuel objected to. Then and there he decided it was not right for a country across the ocean to have so much power in the life of Americans.

Yet Samuel Adams did not look like an agitator. He was a rather short, portly, blue-eyed, mild-mannered, slow-moving, polite man with a nice singing voice. He went to church regularly and was strict about his own and everyone else's morals as long as this did not interfere with his political plans. In many ways he was old-fashioned. Although he wanted America to be rid of England, he was not interested in establishing a country with new ideas. All he wanted was a free nation and one that would exhibit the virtues that he believed had existed among the first Puritan settlers.

Samuel Adams had no part in the actual writing of the Declaration of Independence, but because he had started so early to work for it, he has sometimes been called "the father of independence." He continued in politics all his life, was elected lieutenant governor and then governor of Massachusetts in the 1790's, but his real contribution was in the early years before the war. He died in 1803, at the age of eighty-one, in Boston, the city he had known and loved so well.

Samuel devoted all his energy to politics. After college, he tried business life, but he was not interested and did not do well. He was married twice (his first wife died in 1757), had two children, and although his family seemed happy and devoted, they had to manage much of the time on very little money. Samuel became known as an agitator, a people rouser, or, as the English called him, an "incendiary"—one who starts fires. And indeed, he was behind most of the disturbances and demonstrations in Boston before the war, including the famous Tea Party. He used every means he could find—fair means and often not so fair—to oppose England and to lead the people toward independence.